Cliff Richar

PRIVATE COLLECTI

Edited by PETER FOSS

FIRST PUBLISHED 1989

International Music Publications Limited
Southend Road, Woodford Green
Essex IG8 8HN. England

Music Sales Ltd
8/9 Frith Street
London W7V 5TZ

SOME PEOPLE

Words and Music
by ALAN TARNEY

F
Bbmaj7
2. Some peo-ple they hurt one an-oth-er they love to see
3. Some peo-ple they use one an-oth-er so aim - less-ly
F
Dm7
hurt in the oth-er one's eyes well I'm not like that at all.
not like lov-ers do well I'm not like that at all.
Gm7
Gm7/C
CHORUS
Ab
1.3. Some peo-ple are born
2. Some peo-ple they long
(a)-lone
Dbmaj7
for each oth-er they love to walk
for each oth-er they love to talk
hold - ing the oth-er - one's

Cm7
Fm7
Bbm7
hand they al - ways un - der-stand
Bbm7/Db
Eb
Bbm7/Db
Eb
Bbm7/Db
Eb
some peo - ple cry
some peo-ple know
1.3. F
Bbmaj7
why.
(Oh
F
Bbmaj7
To Coda
)
(Ah Ah)

2.
F
Bbmaj7
why with a word un - spo-ken with a voice un - heard when a thought is
F
bro-ken by a ten - der word when a heart is moved when a heart is
Bbmaj7
D.S. al Coda
thrown the si - lence tells you you're not a -
CODA
Ab
Some peo-ple are born for each oth - er they

D♭maj7
1.
A♭
love to walk hold - ing the oth - er one. Some peo - ple they long
D♭maj7
for each oth-er they love to talk hold - ing the oth-er one.
2.
F
B♭maj7
Hold - ing the oth-er one.
F
B♭maj7
Hold - ing each-oth-er.

WIRED FOR SOUND

Words and Music by
B A ROBERTSON and ALAN TARNEY

Gb
Fm
Eb
ster- e - o
out in the streets, you know.
traf-fic flows
in - to the break - fast show.
what I like
my mu - sic is dy - na-mite.
am-pli - fied
switch - ing to ov - er-drive."
Oh wo
Eb/Db
1-3
2-4
Cm
Bbm
wo wo
(Last time) She said
Oh oh
Ab
Chorus Ab
Ab/C
Eb/Db
Db
Cm/Db
Db
oh.
Pow - er from the nee - dle to the
Cm/Db
Db
Ab
Ab/C
Eb/Db
Db
Cm/Db
Db
Cm/Db
Db
plas - tic A. M. F. M. I feel so ec - sta - tic

Cm
Dbmaj7
Cm
Db
Eb/Db
Db
now, it's mus - ic I've found and I'm wir - ed for
Ab
Ab sus4
To Coda
Ab
D.%. (with repeat) al Coda
CODA
Ab
sound.
Ab
I like small speak - ers, I like tall speak - ers.
Gb/Ab
Ab
(Repeat to Fade)
If they've mus - ic they're wir - ed for sound.

ALL I ASK OF YOU

Music by ANDREW LLOYD WEBBER
Words by CHARLES HART
Additional Words by RICHARD STILGOE

Db
Let me be your free - dom, let day - light dry your tears; I'm
SARAH All I want is free - dom, a world with no more night; and
Dbmaj7
Gb
Cb
Ab/C
here, with you, be - side you, to guard you and to guide you.
you al - ways be - side me, to hold me and to hide me. CLIFF Then
Db
Bbm7
Ebm7
Ab
SARAH Say you love me ev - 'ry wak - ing mo - ment,
say you'll share with me one love, one life - time,
SARAH Say you'll share with me one love, one life - time,
you.)

Db/F Bbm7 Ebm7 /Ab Db Bbm7

turn my head with talk of summer-time.__ Say you need me with you
let me lead you from your so - li - tude__ Say you want me with you
BOTH say the word and I will fol-low you.__ Share each day with me, each

1. Db/F Gb Db/Ab
Ebm7 Ab

To Coda ⊕ *rubato*

now and al - ways, pro-mise me__ that all you say is true,
here be - side you,
night, each morn-ing,

2. Db/F Gb Db/Ab
Ebm7/Ab Ab6 Ebm7/Ab

rall.

that's all I ask of an - y - where__ you go, let me go too,____

D.%. a tempo
al Coda
Ebm7/Ab
Ab6
Ebm7/Ab
that's all I ask of
CODA
Db/F
Gb
Db/Ab
rall.
SARAH say you love me;
CLIFF You know I do;
Ebm7/Ab
Ab6
Ebm7/Ab
Db
Bbm7
Ebm7
Ab
Db/F
Bbm7
a tempo
BOTH Love me, that's all I ask of you.
Ebm7
/Ab
Db
Bbm7
Ebm7
Ab
Db/F
Gb
Db/Ab
Ebm7/Ab
Ab6
Ebm7/Ab
Db
molto rall.
Love me, that's all I ask of you.

CARRIE

Words and Music by
TERRY BRITTEN and BRIAN ROBERTSON

Yeah, may-be it would be bet - ter if I tel - e - phoned. Car - rie does - n't
F F/E D(no 3rd) C D(no 3rd) C
live here an - y - more.__ Car - rie used to room on the sec - ond floor.__
You could al - ways ask at the corn - er store
Dm C Dm C Dm C B♭maj7
1.
__ Sor - ry that she left no for - ward-ing ad - dress that was known to me__
Car - rie had a
C E♭maj9 Fmaj9 B♭/C C/D C/A
2.
Car - rie does - n't date with her own kind of fate, It's plain to see..
Dm C Dm C E♭maj9 Fmaj7 B♭/C C/D D♭/E

D7sus
D
D7sus
D
An-oth-er miss-ing per-son,
One of ma-ny, we as - sume.
C/D
D
C/D
D
F
The young wear their free - dom like cheap_per - fume.
F/E
D(no 3rd)
C
Dm
(It's use-less in-for - ma-tion) Re-turn-ing my call. (To help the sit - u -
C
B♭maj7
C

a - tion) They've noth-ing at all. You're just an - oth - er mes-sage on a pay phone
Bbmaj7 Am Bb C
wall. Car-rie does - n't live here an - y - more. Car - rie used to room on the sec - ond floor.
Dm C Dm C Dm C Dm C Bbmaj7
Sor - ry that she left no for - ward - ing ad - dress that was known to me.
C Ebmaj9 Fmaj9 Bb/C C/D C/A
Dm C Dm Dm/C Dm
3

Bbmaj7 Csus C Eb F Ab Bb
Car-rie does-n't live here an-y-more.
Dm Am Dm C Dm C Dm
— Car-rie used to room on the sec-ond floor. Sor-ry that she
C Dm C Bbmaj7 C
left no for-ward-ing ad-dress. It's a mys-ter-y.
Ebmaj9 Fmaj9 Bb/C C/D Ebmaj7 Dm

REMEMBER ME

Words and Music
by ALAN TARNEY

Moderately, with a strong beat

Cm
G
Cm
you feel this world is to blame, You've been cry — in'.
G
Cm
G
Cm
On - ly, on - ly in-side will you know, But still you won— der
G
Cm
G
some— times Where can, where can you go?—
Cm
D
C
D
Re-mem-ber me, oh, when you feel this way—

C
D
And you need some -one to lean— on.
Ev-er too far a - way,—
And if you're ever
Re-
G
C
To Coda
C
D
I am the one,
I am the one. Re - mem-ber me,— I
mem-ber me
Re - mem-ber me
C
D
G
C
D
am the one— who sees in your eyes.—
Re - mem-ber me,— I
C
D
G
am the one— who sees in your eyes.—

D
C
Re-mem-ber me, I am your guard-ian an— gel And I'll nev - er
C
D
C
D
let you fall.——— And if you're ev-er, ev- er in fear or dan— ger,
Re-
G
C
G
I am the one; I am the one who — will turn,
mem-ber me Re - mem-ber me
Cm
G
Cm
turn all your dark- ness to light, In the morn— in'.

G
Cm
G
Cm
D.𝄋 al 𝄌 Coda
You learn when you're too hard on your - self, You can call —— me.
𝄌 CODA
C
D
C
D
mem - ber me,—— I am the one — who sees
G
C
D
in your eyes.— Re - mem-ber me,— I
C
D
G
Repeat to fade
am the one— who sees in your eyes.— Re-

TRUE LOVE WAYS

Words and Music by
NORMAN PETTY and BUDDY HOLLY

ways.
Through-out the days
Our true love ways
R.H.
Bb Eb Bb
Ebm6
Bb
Will bring us joys to share with those who real - ly care,
Some-times we'll
Db
F C7 F F7
sigh,
Some-times we'll cry,
And we'll know why, just you and
Bb Eb F7 Bb Dm Eb F7 Bb Gm
1.
2.
I, know true_ love_ ways.
Just you know ways.
Cm F7 Bb Eb Bb
Bb Eb Bb

DREAMIN'

Words and Music by
ALAN TARNEY and LEO SAYER

B
Bmaj7
2nd Fret
Here am I, I'm tak-ing a chance in run-ning a-round with stars in my
Here am I, I'm tak-ing a chance I'm walk-in' on air fly-in' so
A
eyes.
high
Here I am, I'm look-ing for you,
Here am I, fac-in' the truth, there's
C#sus4
C#
won-der-ing why do I feel so blue.
no oth-er way I'll ev-er make you mine.
I'm
CHORUS
Db
Gb
dream-in', dream-in' of me and you. I'm dream-in',
dream-in' will see me through. Nev-er let an-y chan-ces pass me by,
Db/Cb

Gb
A
Bsus4
Db
A
B
Db
I'm gon-na dream you right in - to my life,
yeah dream you right in-to my life.
Dream-in',
Gb
Cb
1
Gb
dream-in' will see me through, wom-an, you'd bet - ter be-lieve that I'm dream - in' you in - to my
2
Gb
Db
Gb
in - to my
wom-an,
(life)
you've got to be-lieve me wo-man
oh
Db
Gb
Cb
wom-an
you've got to be-lieve me wom - an
I'll be
dream - in' you
Gb
Db
Gb
Fade on Repeat
in - to my life.
You've got to be-lieve me wom - an.

GREEN LIGHT

Words and Music
by ALAN TARNEY

Eb
Bb7
Eb
Keep-in' my-self —— out of sight
Search-in' for a
[2nd time, instrumental 8 bars]
F
Fm7
green light.
Well I've heard the stor-y be-fore—
F
Fm7
But that won't stop me search—— in'. ——
It's been so long since she
F
gave me a sign,—
A sign to stop my head turn—— ing. ——

Bb
Eb
F
But all I have — are — just your own memories,
Bb
Eb
C7
But you know ba - by, ba - by that's mine,—'Cause I'm spend-in' all— of my time—
1
2
Search-in' for a
Search-in' for a
Repeat to fade
green light From just this side of mid - night.
Search-in' for a

SHE MEANS NOTHING TO ME

Words and Music
by JOHN DAVID

B A E B A E F♯ D
teach her but dar - lin' how much
F♯ B F♯ D G F♯
long - er can I keep on liv - ing this lie
CHORUS
G♯m E F♯ B G♯m E F♯ B
She means no-thing to me she means no-thing to me
G♯m E F♯ G♯m F♯ E
I'm still as free as a bird don't care what you heard a - bout me she means
B A E B A E B A E B A E
no-thing to me no more

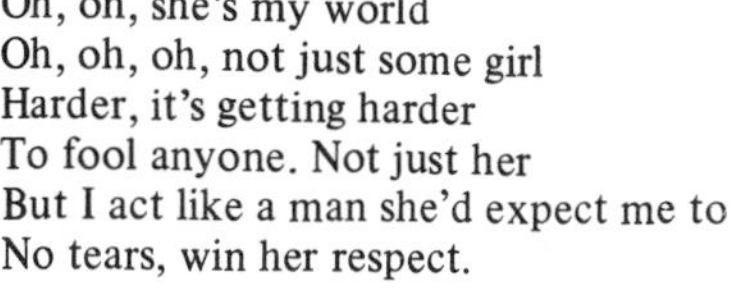

VERSE 2: Oh, oh, she's my world
Oh, oh, oh, not just some girl
Harder, it's getting harder
To fool anyone. Not just her
But I act like a man she'd expect me to
No tears, win her respect.

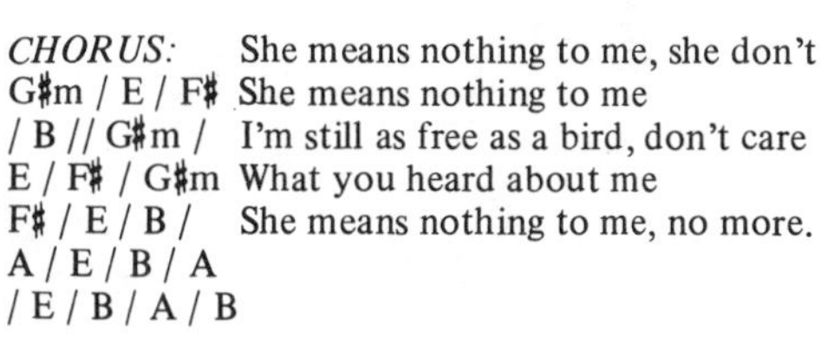

CHORUS: She means nothing to me, she don't
G♯m / E / F♯ She means nothing to me
/ B // G♯m / I'm still as free as a bird, don't care
E / F♯ / G♯m What you heard about me
F♯ / E / B / She means nothing to me, no more.
A / E / B / A
/ E / B / A / B

INSTR: *(Gtr solo* – E / C♯m / G♯m / F♯ / E / C♯m / G♯m / D)

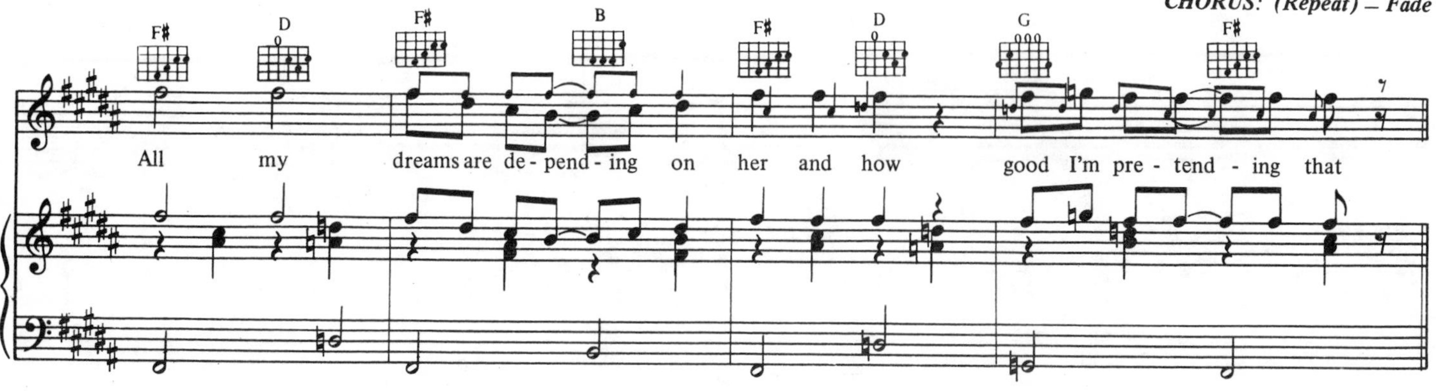

DADDY'S HOME

Words and Music by
JAMES SHEPPARD and WILLIAM MILLER

be by your side! Your best friend's a - round and told me_ you had tear - drops_ in your eyes.
Fm7 Bb7 Eb Cm Fm7 Bb7
Dad - dy's Home, Dad - dy's Home to stay.
Eb Cm Fm7 Bb7 Eb E
It was - n't on a Sun - day, Mon-day and Tues-day went by. It
Eb Eb7 Ab Bb7 Eb
mf
was-n't_ on a Tues - day_ af-ter - noon. All I could do_was cry, But I made a prom - ise_ that you
Fm7 Bb7 Eb Ab Bb7

trea - sure, I made it all back to you. How I
Eb G7 Cm F7 Bb7
wait - ed for this mo-ment to be by your side! Your best friend's a-round and told me you had
Eb Cm Fm7 Bb7 Eb Cm
tear - drops in your eyes. Dad - dy's Home, Dad - dy's Home to
Fm7 Bb7 Eb Cm Fm7 Bb7
1.
2.
stay. You're my stay.
mp
mf
Eb E Fm Bb7 Eb E Eb6

HEART USER

Words and Music by
TERRY BRITTEN and SUE SHIFRIN

G
Em
F
- pec - ca-ble taste. — She'll tell you it runs in her blood. In a
cold heart race. — She's wear-ing that dead - ly per - fume. You must ad -
Dm
Am
Dm7
E7+
cloud of per-fume — she walks in - to the room, — It comes to a stop — when she does. —
mi - re the skill — as he goes in for the kill — It's time to at - tack, — make his move. —
Am
G
Am
G
F
— She's a
He's a
Heart - us-er No time for los-ers
She'll
He'll
use you up and
Am
G
Am
G
Am
G
throw your love a - way - Heart - us - er, a bar - ra -
F
Am
G
1. Am
Dm
cu - da,
She'll
He'll
use you, Just don't get in
her
his
way. —

Am
Dm
Am
2
Am
Dm
He's
Am
G
Am
Where you
Am
Dsus
D
C
been all my life?— This is love at first sight. Could swear we've met some-where be -
Am
Dsus
D
fore. She throws back her head and she shame-less - ly says, "You
C
Em
F
got real good taste, tell me more" And the la - dy in black— thinks she's

G
Em
F
set - ting her trap And he thinks she's play - ing his game. But an - y -
3
Dm
Am
Dm7
bo - dy can tell they're just in - to them-selves, They're two of a kind, They're the
E7+
Am
G
Am
G
same. They're just Heart - us - ers No time for
F
Am
G
Am
G
Am
los - ers They'll use you up and throw your love a - way. Heart - us - ers,
G
F
Am
G
a bar - ra - cu - da, They'll use you, Just don't get in their way.
Repeat and fade

A LITTLE IN LOVE

Words and Music
by ALAN TARNEY

un - der - stand the way you feel, you're just a lit - tle in love (just a
coo I need you so I'm just a lit - tle in love just a
feel - ing just like me just a lit - tle in love (just a
G
Am/G
G
lit - tle) you're just a lit - tle in love. (just a lit - tle)
lit - tle) I'm just a
lit - tle) you're just a
1
Am/G
G
Am/G
2
lit - tle in love. (just a lit - tle)
lit - tle in love (just a lit - tle)
You say you're will-ing to learn,
3
G
Am/G
Bm
F#m/B
C

you need a friend, a friend who will help you, 'cos you're just a lit - tle in
Bm
F♯m/B
C
Am
CHORUS
love oh yeah a lit - tle in love you are
G
Em
C
D
G
Em
a lit - tle in love with some - one you just
C
D
B♭
Gm
like to see, like me, you're in love oh yeah
Am
Bm
G
Em

D.S. (no repeat)
al Coda
To Coda ⊕
a lit - tle in love.
C D G E♭ C B♭ F/B♭
⊕ CODA
oo
you're in love
F/B♭ C D E
(oh yeah) a lit-tle in love
you are a lit-tle in love
A F♯m D E A F♯m D E
Repeat to Fade
with some-one you just like to see
like me, you're in love,
C Am Bm C♯m

WE DON'T TALK ANYMORE

Words and Music
by ALAN TARNEY

Dm
Am
G
F
a long time a - go
you know which way to go
you were the lone - ly one,
you're on your own a - gain
Dm
Am
G
now it comes to let - ting go
don't come cry - in' to me
you are the
when you're the
F
G9
on - ly one
lone - ly one
Do you know what you've done?
re - mem - ber what you've done
CHORUS
G7
C
G/C
C
G/C
C
G/C
Dm/C
It's so fun - ny
how we don't talk
an - y - more.
C
G/C
C
It's so fun - ny

G/C
C
G/C
Dm/C
why we don't talk any-more
but I ain't los - ing sleep
C
Bb/C
F/C
Bb/C
F/C
C/G
G
G/A
and I ain't count - ing sheep.
D/A
A
E/A
A
E/A
A
E/A
Bm/A
It's so fun - ny
how we don't talk
an - y - more.
(last time repeat to Chorus & fade ad lib.)
C
G/C
C
G/C
C
G/C
Dm/C
1
2
D.S.
Well it

NEVER SAY DIE

Words and Music by
TERRY BRITTEN and SUE SHIFRIN

hide, go seek, Don't let the grass grow un - der your feet. Get out,— get up,
Am Am7 Am Dm7 G7 Am
— get on,— get mov-ing out, Don't sur-ren - der, Don't give up the fight. You give a
Dm G7 Dm G G6
lit - tle bit more If you want her back— it's a full at - tack. You give a
Am F G11 C/G
lit - tle bit more. If you want to win— you don't give in— You give a
3
Am Fmaj9 Dm9 Dm7 G

to Coda
lit - tle bit more. When you think you're through what you got to do is give a
Am
F
F6
G
1.
lit - tle bit more.
Am
D7
C/G
D
2.
lit - tle bit more.
F
G
G7
Fmaj7
G
Don't give up the fight, Got to keep on go - ing with all your might.
Am

Try hard, don't stop. Got to keep on giv-ing it all you got.
Nev-er give up, nev-er give up, nev-er say die. Be - lieve in I,— you can
reach the top— got to give it a shot. Don't— say no, got to get in the flow.
D
C
D
Am7
D
Am7

So don't hide, go seek Don't
D
Am7 Am Am7 Am Am9
crawl a - way, get back on your feet. Get out, get up,
Dm7 G7
Am
get on, get mov - ing out. Don't sur - ren - der.
Dm G7 Dm Dm7 G
D.S. al Coda
Don't give up the fight. You give a
G6
CODA
D.S. and fade
lit - tle bit more. You give a
Am
G

THE ONLY WAY OUT

Words and Music
by RAY MARTINEZ

D
E
A
D/A
1 E/A
A
ly way in and it's you.
2. I've been
2 E/A
A
Em7
A
I spent a lot of time at the cross -
Em7
A
roads get - ting that lone - ly feel - ing in - side
C♯m
F♯m
sud - den - ly you stopped the rain

C♯m F♯m D E

you changed the view now eve - ry - where's lead - ing to you. —

3. Let's

VERSE 3: Let's get this thing going let's move it along
Let me do all the things I've been missing so long.
'Cause the only way out is the only way in and it's you.

VERSE: (Instr.)

MIDDLE: I spent a lot of time at the crossroads
Getting that lonely feeling inside
Suddenly you made the rescue you pulled me through
Now let me do something for you.

(Link chords: E/F♯)

[KEY: B]

VERSE 4: Let's get this thing going let's move it along
Let's do all the things I've been missing so long.
And the only way out is the only way in and it's you,
Yeah the only way out is the only way in and it's you,
Yeah the only way out is the only way in and it's you.

INTRO: (Repeat) + The only way out
It's the only way in
It's the only way out
It's the only way in . . . . .
(FADE)

LITTLE TOWN

Words and Music arranged
by CHRISTOPHER EATON

Bb
Bbsus4
Bb
F
Bb
— thy deep — and — dream - less sleep
— im - parts — to — hu - man hearts
F
Eb
the — si - lent — stars go
the — bless - ings — of His
Bb
F
Eb
F
Eb
F/Eb
by.
heav - en.
1. Yet in thy
2. We hear the
3. No ear may
Eb
F/Eb
Eb
F/Eb
Eb
F/B
dark — streets — shin - eth the ev - er - last - ing light,
Christ - mas — ang - els the great glad tid - ings tell,
hear — His — com - ing but in this world of sin,

Eb
F/Eb
the hopes and fears of all the years are met in
O come to us a - bide with us, Our Lord Em -
where meek souls will re - ceive Him still the dear Christ
Fsus4
1 2
F/Bb
Eb/Bb
Bb
thee to - night.
an - u - el.
en - ters
3
Fade
in.
Twin-kle twin - kle lit - tle star now I know just what you are.

SUDDENLY

Words and Music
by JOHN FARRAR

Slowly

F Bb Bb⁰ F/A Db/Ab Gb F

Bb Cm7 Ab Bb

HE She walks in —— and I'm sud-den-ly a he - ro.

Ebm Cb Db

I'm tak - en in, —— my hopes be-gin —— to —— rise. ——

Dbmaj7 Dm7 Bb C11 Fm7

SHE Look at me, Can't you tell —— I'd be so Thrilled —— to see ——

Db Csus C Csus C7

the message in your eyes. ——

HE You make it seem-I'm so close-to my dream-And then sud —— den-ly it's all

Fmaj7 Dm7 B♭maj7 Am Gm Dm
SHE
BOTH
there. Sudden-ly the wheels are in mo— tion— And I - I - I - I I'm ready to sail—
B♭maj7 B♭6 C7 Fmaj7 Dm7 B♭maj7 Am Gm Dm
an-y o— cean.— Sud-den-ly— I don't need the an— swers— 'Cos I - I - I - I—
B♭maj7 B♭m F B♭
I'm rea-dy to take all my chan— ces— with you.
B♭o F/A D♭/A♭ G♭ F B♭
Cm7 A♭ B♭ E♭m
HE
How can I feel you're all that mat-ters. I, I'd re-ly— on

C♭
D♭maj7
an - y-thing —— you —— say.
Dm7
B♭
C11
Fm7
SHE
I'll take care that no il-lu- sions —— shat-ter If —— you dare ——
D♭
Csus
C
Csus
C7
HE
to say what you should say. You make it seem–I'm so close – to my dream–And then sud —— den-ly it's all
Fmaj7
Dm7
B♭maj7
Am
Gm Dm
SHE
BOTH
there. Sudden-ly —— the wheels are in mo — tion —— And I - I - I - I —— I'm ready to sail–
B♭maj7
B♭6
C7
Fmaj7
Dm7
B♭maj7
Am
Gm Dm
—— an-y o —— cean. — Sud-den-ly —— I don't need the an — swers — 'Cos I - I - I - I —

TO CODA
Bbmaj7
Bbm
F
Bb
I'm ready to take all my chan- ces with you.
Bb0
F/A
Db/Ab
Gb
F
Am/E
Dm7
F/C
Bbm
Ebm6
Db
HE
Why do I feel so a - live when you're near? There's no way an-y hurt can get
F7sus
F7
Bbmaj7
Bb7
Eb
BOTH
through. Long-ing to spend ev-'ry mo-ment of the day with you, with
C7
Fmaj7
Dm7
D.S. al CODA
you. Sud-den-ly the wheels are in mo-
CODA
Bb0
F

SLOW RIVER

Words and Music by
ELTON JOHN and BERNIE TAUPIN

G/A
D
like you used to do.
like a wild dog.
But
I still
D
C/D
C
you don't re - men - ber things like that, do you? The bal-ance was un - ev - en but I'm
see your eyes to-night like head-lights through the fog, but one foot in your door, oh that's
G/A
D
break - ing through.
all I ev - er got.
C
G
D
C
G
F
G
Slow ri-vers run cold, shal-low wat - ers ne-ver sank so low.

Bb
C
G
D
F/C
C
I thought I'd drown and you'd
ne-ver
know, you're a
slow
ri-ver and you
run
so
G
D
1.
2.
cold.
The
G/B
C
D
chan-ces
are
you'll
re
-
ap-pear.
Swim my
way
in
a
flood
Em
F
G
of
tears,
no place
to
hide
your con
-
science
so
you're
a
sink -

C
D
C
G
- ing ship — with no place to go. Slow ri - vers run
D
C
G
F
G
B♭
cold, shal-low wat - ers ne-ver sank so low. I thought I'd drown and you'd
1.
C
G
D
F/C
C
G
ne-ver know, you're a slow ri - ver and you run so cold.
2.
D
F/C
C
G
D
slow ri - ver and you run so cold.
molto rall.
a tempo

PLEASE DON'T FALL IN LOVE

Words and Music
by MIKE BATT

Slow ballad tempo

F
C
F
C
F#dim
I was a-way — And now that it's hap — pened I just want to say — That I'm
C
G7
Ab
C
beg-ging you, Ba — by, Please don't fall in — love. —
I'm
We
Am
us - ual - ly strong — But I'm feel - ing so weak, — It
kissed at the air — port, We said we could wait, — I be-lieve —
Bb
wells up in - side — me, I cry when I speak. — But the
— it is we — Who de-ter — mine our fate; — And I

C
E7
Am
C7
more I call you on the phone, The more I feel a-lone,—
love you more than I can say Don't throw it all a-way,—
F
Dm
1 G7sus
G7
2 G7sus
G7
— And the less we have to say.— I
— Don't let it go by.— — I
F
C
F
C
know that you're with— him Just now as I write,— I
F
C
F#dim
C
know you need some—one To hold you at night,— But I'm beg-ging you, Ba— by,

G7
C
Dm
Gsus
G
Please don't fall in love. I
F
C
F
C
F
C
know you don't tell— me To spare me the pain,— Don't want you to tell— me, I
F♯dim
C
G7
don't need his name,— But I'm beg-ging you, Ba— by, Please don't fall in—
ritard.
Slow
A♭
C
D♭
C
love.—
dim.

MY PRETTY ONE

Words and Music
by ALAN TARNEY

To Coda
3rd time
1.
D
be here with you, my pret - ty one.
you and on - ly you, my pret - ty one.
com - pare with you, my pret - ty one.
2.
D
Pret - ty one,
G
I long to hold you, through the night
F♯m
I want to hold
you, pret-ty one
G
has no one told you, I love

D
G
you.
An - y day
and you will find
F♯m
me full of joy
when you're be - side me,
in a mo -
G
A
ment like this could it be
what I've missed all my life.

3.
D
G
Well I love your smile and I love your eyes
And I need you now as I write this song,
A
G
and the way you talk makes me feel so nice nothing can com - pare
did I hear you say you're the on - ly one from a lone - ly prayer
1.
A
with the way you are, oh,
I am in the air.

2.
A
D.%. al Coda
(With Repeats)
CODA
D
A
No, no - thing can com - pare with,
D
com - pare with you, my pret - ty one.

OCEAN DEEP

Words and Music by
RODNEY TROTT and JONATHAN SWEET

Cm7
Fsus4
F
B♭
ask, a lit - tle kind - ness in the night.
ask, a lit - tle sad - ness when you go.
ask, a lit - tle feel - ing when we touch.
F/A
Dm
F7/C
Please don't leave me be - hind, no, don't tell me love is
May - be you need a friend, on - ly please don't let's pre -
Why am I still a - lone? I've got a heart with - out a
Gm
E♭maj7
Cm9
blind. A lit - tle love is all I ask, and that is
tend. A lit - tle love is all I ask, and that is
home. A lit - tle love is all I ask, and that is
F
1 Fsus4
F
2
Gm
all. ooh.
all. I wan - na spread my wings
all.

Ebmaj7
Cm7
but I just can't fly, as a string of pearls and pret-ty girls
Eb
F
rall.
Eb/F
F
Eb/F
F
Bb
A tempo
go sail - ing by. Oc - ean deep,
Ebmaj7
F/Eb
Dm7
I'm so a - fraid to show my feel - ings, I have sailed a mil - lion ceil-
Gm
Eb
F/Eb
Bb/D
F/C
Bb
Eb
A tempo
- ings in my sol - i - ta - ry room. Oc - ean deep,
poco rall.

Bb
Ebmaj7
F/Eb
Dm7
will I ev - er find a love?
May - be she has found an -
Gm
Eb
F/Eb
oth - er, and as I cry my - self to sleep
Bb/D
Eb
F
To Coda
Fsus4
F
D.C.
I know this love of mine will keep, oc - ean
CODA
Gm/F
F7
Bb
A tempo
F/Bb
oc - ean deep, I'm so
Poco rall.

Eb
F/Eb
Bb/D
Eb
lone - ly, lone - ly lone - ly.
F
Bb/D
F/C
Bb
Eb
A tempo
Bb
Oc - ean deep,
Poco rall.
on my own in my room
I'm so lone-ly oh so lone-ly
Eb
F/Eb
Dm7
I'm so lone -
Gm
Eb
F/Eb
Bb/D
F/C
Repeat to Fade
Bb
- ly.
Oc - ean
3

SHE'S SO BEAUTIFUL

Words and Music
by HANS POULSEN

Moderate beat

Dm
C
Dm
C
Trial and er— ror true,—
Oh, if you were to vis— it there—
Gsus4
G
C♯dim
You would love— her too.
She's so
Dm7
G7
C
Am
beau - ti -ful,—
She's so kind and free,—
She's so
Dm7
G7
Gsus4
C
beau - ti - ful,— She's all there is— to me.

Am7
C♯dim
Dm7
G7
C
She's so beau - ti-ful,—
She's so kind and free,—
Am
Dm7
G7
Gsus4
Csus4
She's so beau - ti - ful,— She's all —— there is— to me.—
1
2
C♯dim
She's so
Dm7
G7
C
beau - ti - ful,—
She's so kind and free,—

Am
Dm7
G7
Gsus4
C
She's so beau-ti-ful,— She's all — there is— to me.——
Am7
C♯dim
Dm7
G7
C
She's so beau - ti - ful,— She's so kind and free,—
Am
Dm7
G7
Gsus4
She's so beau - ti - ful,— She's all —— there is— to me.——
Csus4
C♯dim
Repeat to fade
She's so

TWO HEARTS

Words and Music
by ALAN TARNEY

A D/A A D/A Em D/A A
heart, the same love, on the night you be - gan, meant ev - 'ry -
A D/A A D/A Em D/A Em A
thing, clos-est thing that your heart ev - er had. Dreams
A D/A A D/A Em D/A A
change, change your heart, and in-ter - fere with your plans. The same
go now you're free, free to go where you please. But when you're
A D/A A D/A Em D/A Em A
heart, the same love are noe out of your hands.
free all you hear is your lone - ly heart beat.
When two

A/D
D
A
hearts drift a - way you can hear voi-ces say that the
A/D
D
Em
real dia-mond ring did - n't ev - er real - ly mean a thing. When two
A/D
D
A
hearts drift a - way, a lone - ly voice be-gins to say there's no
A/D
Em
To Coda
room for an - y - one, but you're think - ing no more what you've done.

1.
2.
You can
G
C
Bb
Dm
G
C
Bb
Dm
F
G
D.%. al Coda
CODA
When two
The same

A
heart, the same love, on the night you be - gan, meant ev - 'ry
thing, clos - est thing that your heart ev - er
D
A
had.
G/D
D
A
Repeat to Fade

MISTLETOE AND WINE

Words by LESLIE STEWART and JEREMY PAUL
Music by KEITH STRACHAN

F
F7
E♭
passed, there's a new —— be - gin-ning. Dreams of San - ta,
B♭
C7sus(9)
F7
dreams of snow, Fin - gers numb, fac - es a - glow. It's
B♭
Christ - mas time, mis-tle-toe and wine, Child - ren
E♭
B♭
F
F7
sing - ing Chris - ti-an rhyme With logs on the fire — and

B♭
gifts on the tree; A time to re - joice in the good that we
B♭
see. 2. A time —— for liv - ing, a time for be - liev - ing, A
3. It's a time —— for giv - ing, a time for get - ting, A
Gm E♭ Gm F F7
time —— for trust-ing, not —— de - ceiv - ing.
time for —— for - giv-ing, and for —— for - get - ting.
E♭ B♭
Love and laugh - ter and joy ev - er af - ter;
Christ-mas is love, Christ-mas is peace; A

Printed in Great Britain by Hobbs the Printers of Southampton 3/93